STAR IN THE EYE

James Shea

Cover design by   Suzanne E. Fedea
Cover art by   Parker Smathers
Book design by   Rebecca Wolff

Published in the United States by   Fence Books
                                             Science Library 320
                                             University at Albany
                                             1400 Washington Avenue
                                             Albany, NY 12222
                                             www.fenceportal.org

Fence Books are distributed by   .   University Press of New England
                                             www.upne.com

and printed in Canada by   Westcan Printing Group
                                             www.westcanpg.com

Library of Congress Cataloguing in Publication Data
        Shea, James [1976–]
        Star in the Eye/James Shea

Library of Congress Control Number: 2008934249

ISBN 1-934200-14-X

ISBN 13: 978-1-934200-14-8

FIRST EDITION

Grateful acknowledgement is made to the following publications in which the poems in this book first appeared: *American Letters and Commentary, Bird Dog, Black Clock, Boston Review, Bridge Magazine, The Canary, Columbia Poetry Review, Court Green, Crazyhorse, Crowd, Gulf Coast, GutCult, jubilat, LIT, Machine Made, MiPOesis Magazine, Mrs. Maybe, Pindeldyboz, Verse,* and *Word For/ Word.* "Haiku" appeared in *Isn't It Romantic: 100 Love Poems by Younger American Poets* (Wave Books, 2004).

FENCE BOOKS are published in partnership with the University at Albany and the New York State Writers Institute, and with help from the New York State Council on the Arts and the National Endowment for the Arts.

STAR IN THE EYE

James Shea

WINNER OF THE FENCE MODERN POETS SERIES
SELECTED BY NICK FLYNN

Albany, NY

For my family

CONTENTS

TURNING AND RUNNING

The sun was backing away from me,
slowly, like one I have betrayed.
So I ran to the river to burn in it.
And they blocked the road with ambulances.

They gave me surgery on my mouth.
My eyes were packed with feathers,
and my whole face was painted flat.
An expert told me I was probably a joke.

There were at least four things
I should have said. Do not step on the rug
with the live birds sewn into it.

PARTS OF AN INLAND PIER

The boys lie open for a snowfall.

I don't want to be here for that.

The two boys turn their heads to me.

A thunder-sound somersaults in the sky.

Will they heal? Will they be *better*?

I drove with my jeep to the beach.

The waves in general were special to me.

I saw them all for a moment at a time.

The two boys woke to their deaths.

They could not give up more.

There is no rhetoric of a storm.

There will be a way to explain what I am saying.

I woke to three geese flying in a loose v.

I could live my whole life right here, in this chair.

SHORT SHORT

Swimming and tanning are two hobbies
of mine. This winter I'm going to see
at least ten million snowflakes.
I have this dream where I pretend
to swim in the air with my hands.
And I'm in a carnival. And a minnow
circles my thigh, too. Then someone
tells the policeman in shorts.
I think sunfish swim without even knowing it.
I saw these waves that seemed plastic.
Love consists mostly of timing
and cleanliness. (I made that up!)
I thought the cat sounded like
a trumpet for a minute. I remember
about 10 years ago when I was
in the army, the sergeant told everybody
to find the low point in the day
and wait there. What a jerk!
What's going on now? Tell me
when you want to see that ornament.
I know a girl who looks like a famous swimmer
from the '50s. Hey, seriously,
I saw this tree break in a storm.
Is that somebody snoring or some kind
of recording device? It must be expensive.

AROUND THE WIND

You are the performance artist
who charges people to leave.

You were having an affair with the sky.
You filmed as much as you could.

I can't imagine any wish without a stain.
There was a shiny animal in the street

that ran at my legs. I called out to it, Ryan.
I get in a plane and look for the earth.

I am without the sight of existence for miles.
I can see nothing from all sides.

Do you hear that plane in the sky?
It sounds like the motor went out.

There was heavy heavy snow. Time passed by.
I would land a plane on your street.

PANOPLIES

You are not free to enjoy the nostalgia.
Don't look at me. The oncoming traffic
we listen: a man crawls out of an argument.
I keep saying, I saw him, I saw him.
I am not laughing with every part of myself.
You continue drinking being smart enough.
I built this house from scratch. I am not
going to repeat myself. You tell me.
We are born a thousand times without hands.
I never answered the question. I am going
to eat this sandwich. I need an excuse.
You burn the sheets and knife the bed.
I left something with everyone I met tonight.
I sleep with my fingers under the pillow.

IDEA OF A MUTINY

The girls in groups
would not give me
their walkie-talkies.

I made a question
and brought it to the shore.

The only way I knew
how to get there was to think
I had gone too far
and to keep going.

The sea sort of gleeked on me.

Then I saw my dog
wake up last night—
barking, defending everything
from everything else.

BROKEN CLOUD

Broken Cloud couldn't erase his answers
without raising the paper to the lamp,
shading his impressions with a pencil
of his own. Broken Cloud tried to avoid
incorporating lies into his response.
He narrowed himself into a singularity,
a not-turning-away-from-it.
He quickly made a mistake and put on
his younger brother's shoes and went out.
He did not like his fat voice.
Broken Cloud approached the lodestar.

MECHANICAL FOLIAGE

I felt the rapid turning of the sun in my direction.
I never saw this many squirrels at once.

A young entrepreneur sold me his business card.
He told me this was one of the beautiful days.

He offered a presentation on my whereabouts:
half of you awake, the other half was not asleep.

He said I would see handsome epiphanies,
a vision unifying the particulars, for example.

He put his hand up my sleeve and touched my chest.
In other words, it was a dream I still remember.

I heard sheets of ice clink over the lake.
I found the extraordinary moment and recorded it.

I wash small trees with my hands, sponging
the trunk and leaves. I live once supposedly.

STORMS

I am Kumi. This is Ken.
Is this your bag? Is that
a school? You are Tarō.
Are you Emiko? What is this?
I play shōgi. I do not like
tempura. Do you play the piano?
Is this a pen or a pencil?
What do you play? I have
many books. Clean your room.
Don't use a pen. Let's play tennis.
This yukata is beautiful.
These are eggs. Those are eggs.
Who is that girl? This is
my bike. That is my father's bike.
Whose pen is this? I know Billy.
I like him. I know Ann.
I like her. They like Ann.
She likes them. Where is Pat?
I can speak English. I can't swim.
Can you swim? Yes, I can.
No, I can't. Which do you speak,
English or Japanese? Billy is playing
tennis. Is Ann playing tennis?
What time is it? Did you write poems?
Yes, I did. No, I didn't.

REPLICAS OF GRACE

It's in-approximate
like a cyclone
but easy to follow.

I do tremble
between a number
and its numeral.

I feel more north.
I never move.

I see a ladder
I did not make.

CRISES

The chamber envelops you deftly
it takes you in even the you

you thought you had lost the way
an automobile embraces all its

passengers it's so thoroughgoing
as when one masters something

or someone and perhaps you have
mastered me as you know the hock

of my horse and indeed I did not
attend the rally but rather stood

yards away near the oak stump (cut
last year) and watched everyone

forced to enjoy the failed parade and
every morning I wake up of course

and rise from bed and begin to shave.

*

Even in the grandest monuments lifted
what remains something always

seemingly into the stratosphere
something of the architect remains

married to the soil remains inside
of him he cannot ever build it all

out of himself for he does not even
have familiarity of the materials no

he constructs these blueprints orders
their completion and still something

stays behind irretrievable but some
comfort in that it cannot ever all

be expunged some comfort in the undoable.

*

These are the lay days while we wait
for something beyond ourselves but

which includes ourselves to impart
some vision to our crew about to return

across the waters past the simple-minded
monsters who put all of themselves

into their attacks and subsequently feel
defeated even if their swipes reach our hull

because so earnestly they believe
their violence their splaying out

of themselves somehow releases them
from the depths and when the channeled

silvery waters guide you out they require
your trust albeit brief for some other sun

available to you which acts convincingly
which serves as the vital beginning.

THE RIVERBED

On the Riverbed

A bed of rivers—
Feet first down the
Dark blue canyon.

Autumn Riverbed

The shadows of leaves
Look like submerged battleships
In the riverbed.

Family of Riverbeds

O Riverbed! Do you
Have a brother? Some relative
I have yet to meet?

Riverbed Water

A tree tells the river,
The mountains bend for you,
I've seen it. But the river
Does not listen. It is busy
Threading itself forward.

Lonely Riverbed

The riverbed did not have a name.
So the birds called it Land of New Water.

Generous Riverbed

Where two riverbeds join,
There is room
For a larger river.

Egyptian Riverbed

The light in the riverbed
Is like the inner rooms
Of a pyramid,
Lit by torches.

Stone Thrown in a Riverbed

The riverbed is so muddy
It cannot be seen.
For a moment,
We must believe
There is a riverbed.

Why Are You a Riverbed?

An accomplice of the night,
The darkened river overtakes the sky.

Italian Riverbed

Gathered along the riverbed,
She walked among us
Like a cameraman
At a wedding.

Original Riverbed

Fishing
Outside the riverbed, a man
Feeds worms to his penis.

Lovers by the Riverbed

They were confused and happy.
Her cigarette was a white raven
Flying into her mouth!

Riverbed Without Water

It is the dry season.
Not the season of full-stomachs.

Little Riverbed

Does the bed make room for the river?
Or the river for the bed?

Ignoring the Riverbed

A boy by the riverbed
Turns his back to the river.
His body is reflected by the surface.

Riverbed on a Leash

The leash moves
Around the sitting dog.

Safe Riverbed

The clouds are
White and gray—
Like smoke
From a burning, upper sky.

Tao Riverbed

A river is like the Tao.
If you point to the river
It ceases to be a river.
But if you point to the riverbed,
It is still a riverbed.

Woman at the Riverbed

What is that
In the riverbed? A plum?
A baby tooth?

Impossible Riverbed

A tadpole resting
In the riverbed.
Breathing inside water!

Defined Riverbed

"The channel in which
A river flows
Or formerly flowed."

Japanese Riverbed

Near the riverbed, two foreigners
Pretend not to see each other.

Everywhere Riverbed

The riverbed is shallow.
Here it is deep.

Floating Riverbed

I rest in the river (bed).
Fish carry me to sleep!

New England Riverbed

Fashionable antelopes
Feel accomplished—
Drinking at the riverbed.

Riverbed Full of Onions

Can the river return to its source?
Change its watery-mind?

Mistranslated Riverbed

"Recently
I am particularly
Anxious
About you."

Borrowed Riverbed

Reading Stevens and Koch, these
Are the poems we want to write,
The river we want to join.

A Salmon's Riverbed

The salmon swim up
The river—a lone salmon
Hides near a rock
Unable to go on.

Origami Riverbed

A child made a riverbed
Out of paper.
Then he laid it
On the river.

Introspective Riverbed

The riverbed remembered the days
When it had no water.

Doubting Riverbed

I've always been confident
Of my doubts—
Wading in the riverbed.

Upside-Down Riverbed

In the riverbed, the rocks
Are like the tops of

People's heads. So many problems
Underwater!

Echoes of a Riverbed

I am miles from
A riverbed. A bird flies
The distance between us
A hundred times.

Dreaming Riverbed

Night is like a riverbed.
It is a place to sleep
And move. And to move
While sleeping.

Crossing the Riverbed

The duck
Plays with the river—
Knowing it could fly.

A Child's Riverbed

Genius
Is
Always
Instantaneous.

Deceptive Riverbed

Mud in the riverbed
Stirs like brown shadows fighting.
The fish are sciamachists!

Revised Riverbed

A man feeds his penis
To the fish.

Personal Riverbed

The water in the riverbed
Goes around that rock
Like a man
Who thinks he knows his wife.

Julie's Riverbed

Her face was apples
And festive-youth,
Her face was clear
And struck a new
Light as the lamppost
Bowed to her.

Further Down the Riverbed

Her face was
Shriveled like a leaf
On an ocean liner.

Symphony of Riverbeds

Piano in the forest:
A note ricochets off a tree—
Into a leaf's mitochondria.

Penultimate Riverbed

The riverbed
Is a window
With rain
Running
Down
It.

Baby Blue

After the movie
About riverbeds,
You said, I wonder
What it would be like
To be married.
I said, Yes!

HAIKU

Upon Kissing You After You Vomited.
Upon Walking You Home and You Pissing
in Your Pants. Upon Asking a Complete Stranger
about Our Situation. Upon Reading Issa's
Prescripts "Issa in a State of Illness,"
"At Being Bewildered on Waking" and Realizing
the Haiku Poets Were Not So Laconic and How
Could They Be? Poem Before Dying. Poem
Shortly Before I Head to Dinner. Poem in Which
I Enter Drops of Dew Like a Man with Tiny Keys.
Hitomaro has a poem called On Seeing
the Body of a Man Lying Among the Stones
on the Island of Samine in Sanuki Province.
Kanyu's short poem is called A Poem
Shown to My Niece Sonshō on Reaching
the Barrier of the Ran After Being Relegated
to an Inferior Position. Poem Louis Aragon
Would Be Proud Of. Poem I'll Never Show You.
Poem Written in a Bugs Bunny Cartoon as the
Plane's Controls Come Off in My Hands. Poem
that Jerks Around Like a Hamster in a Bag. Bashō
wrote a haiku for his students that he claimed
was his death poem. The night before
he said that for the last 20 years every poem
he had written had been his death poem. Upon
No Longer Recalling My Thoughts When I Was a Boy
Within My Father's Stare. At Being Exhausted
at Having to Explain Why Using Slang

Is More Fun Than Reading a Dictionary of Slang.
The poet Saikaku once wrote 23,500 verses
in 24 hours. Bashō saw Mt. Nikkō and said,
"I was filled with such awe that I hesitated
to write a poem." Upon Looking Past You
into the Mattress, into the Faces of Prior Lovers.
Upon Trying to Cultivate My Inner Life While
also Killing My Ego. On Watching
a 200 pd. Endangered Orangutan
Rape My Wife While She Shouts at Me
Not to Shoot Him. On Seeing a Bloodshot
Spanish Boy Who Was Not Even Crying He Was So Sad
and Not Even Crying He Was So Sad. Poem
in Which I Embody a Moment So Vividly, So
Succinctly, Yet Decorate It with Such Sills,
Such Elaborations. Upon Doodling Your Name
Which Became Your Face Emerging From Day-Old
Coals. Upon Reading that Bashō Believed "A Haiku
Revealing 70 to 80% of Its Subject Is Good, Yet
Those Revealing 50 to 60% Will Never Bore Us."
On Finally Leaving My Attic and Hearing English
for the First Time in 20 Years and It Sounding
Like an Animal's Cry Before It Attacks. Poem
in Response to Flying all the Way to Rome
to Meet You and Being Dumped at the Airport.
Poem about the Next Two Weeks We Spent Together.
Poem as I Sit on This Curb with My Head
in My Hands. Poem After Learning the Japanese
Word for the Simultaneous Feeling of Love
and Hatred. Poem for the Mountain at the End
of My Street. Poem in Response to Some of My
Recent Poems that Seem to Have Been Written
Inside an Aquarium. On Spending a Week in Silence

at a Monastery and Not Being Allowed Pen or Paper.
On Meditating and Feeling Like I Was a Blue Flame.
On Getting Up and Scribbling Something in the Bathroom.
On Stopping at the Train Tracks and Having a Deer
Break His Head Through My Passenger Window,
Stare at Me, and Then Run Back into the Wood.

OPENING ON THE DANCE FLOOR

Do you have a name? These are dark lakes.
Are these dark lakes? A name has you.

Am I half-serious? There's room on the dance floor.
Is there room on the dance floor? I'm half-serious.

Who is he? Monkeys climb trees.
Does a monkey climb trees? I am not him.

Where will you go? The cups are gone.
Are the cups gone? You will go.

Do fish swim? I may kiss you.
May I kiss you? Fish swim and swim.

THIS IS NOT WHAT I CAME HERE FOR

Yesterday and today have me in common.
This could be April in which the rain
breaks up the air that surrounds us.
What are you reading now? The funeral
was postponed and I called everyone.
The people here are really watching television.
When I smell you I cannot smell anything.
Would this CD change me? Or a cup of tea?
I do not know what you are doing.
That was me five years ago and who was he?
I am a lost storm. I am an asian lamp?
That sandal seems to fit you perfectly.
Were you listening and thinking about me
this whole time? The more breakfasts
I make, the more I expect it from myself.

TWO-WAY EXIT

We could only speak to each other.
We were in some kind of weather chamber.

I was sleeping when you asked me.
Were you? No, you were a flammable second.

It was late. Where were you? Not my confidant.
Clouds rained overhead, and we were ,

being rained upon. I forgot about my "audience."
A crow flew itself against the window.

The fog came down around us. The outline
of my hand was clear. The cicadas in the fog

were clear. The fog made certain things,
feelings clearer. You spelled a word on my thigh.

I spoke to you then, so I could speak
to you now: we didn't exist for an instant.

POEM

I was sad I was not the young boy
who passed me each day the way

water carries a ship, but I was happy
I saw him and this contradiction

saddened me, but I was pleased with myself
for having noticed it. I said, Hello—

this startled him and worried me,
but I felt as one who waits

to unfold from a crowded train:
unsure where to go but having the time

to be unsure. We took a picture
together and he left for grade school

and I left for the States. I remember
his funny stroll and his curiosity

at the shop windows and the cars parked
in his way along the sidewalk. They

were less obstructions and more examples
of how the world protrudes out at one.

I have my picture that distorts us, of course,
but what I recall most now are thoughts

of her then and our decision to never
speak again. Why do I say it like this now

to myself? I regret not sleeping with her
the way one regrets not stealing

an umbrella. I remember the seashells
she gave to me and the ones she kept.

I remember trying to kiss her on the bridge
and her smiling like it was a joke.

What are the limits here? The lesson
from the boy? I'm thinking—

a cloak of birds leaving a tree,
an empty field shorn for my welcoming.

UNPERFECTABLE

As you suggested, the beauty
of the house amazed me. It was sleeting now.
But that was okay. The trees
had already prepared for winter.

From then on I wanted advice daily.
I thought I missed the quarter-
colored sky and felt restricted
by a natural, beautiful event.
But it was semi-logical
you said. Like a mystery
I knew how to perceive.

You showed me how when
a storm comes it belongs to everyone.
And when we met, we drank
immediately. In the same sense,
you said yellow is the color of sunflowers,
sunflowers equal summer and summer
equals freedom from troubles.

Later my son said, Hey, you pain me.
My heart is a discrepancy. And I
left for your house and you said
how you wouldn't really say that.
How we draw ourselves back like strings.
My new life needs a new death.
How I keep a little of this one left.

SNOW ENGINE

That evening an incredible
delivery of energy: we folded open
the couch to get at the bed.

I pressed myself into a mirror.
I should have shoveled the entire walk.
I saw myself as a summary of water.

Here, place me wherever.

I made up the whole thing
to protect the animals. They were dying
and I never really let them die.

STOIC WRECK

1

Often two people must separate
to reveal they are inseparable.

There are human, universal moments in a sitcom.

You wake at night rushing to the door,
touching it with your hands.

2

Come here, where one can sit
and feel something. I'm working on a symphony
that uses every instrument.

It sounds like earrings under the carpet.
It's called Stephanie.

3

First, you are alone. You are the last person
that swimmer ever spoke to in his life.

Ideally, you want to become shoreless.

You back away into the light.
You are the One-Who-Fights-Shadows.

FIRST REQUIEM

The cloudy banker left the conversation
as it began to swim through the mouths

of those who stood, gaping. They secured it
inside themselves, winding it tightly,

so tiny, they believed it wasn't there.
The cloudy banker flew into the dawn-lit air,

praying to the patron saint of oblivion.
Some stranger asked, what does it *mean*?

Some still woke each morning to those
who died. Some slept through prose.

Some had to sail to the center of a lake.
And then row back to shore.

RUNAWAY MODEL

I dropped my soulish thingy in the parking lot.
Returning at night, it was gone. I walked home
alone and sleepy.

                        I had a dream about you.
That's, like, a monthly occurrence—how are things?
I hope you're well. I want to speak my mind,
but not put you to sleep with boredom.

This is difficult to explain, but I felt
like the commander had de-pantsed me
and everyone in the barracks was walking past,
creating these small currents of air
that wove themselves fabulously into a wind
coming at my face and my shoulders.

                          Okay, I'm back.
I get lost on my way home from work.
That's the remarkable thing about me.
I am not a hawk that can swim.

THE YELLOWSTONE REVOLUTION

I just realized my recent error: no space/time.
In this way, a bird rides its bike into me.
Shavings of my teeth fall off into my mouth.

This is my first life and I want to get it right.
Some commercial for death? That hermit can blow
a miniature version of himself into the air.

This is a pickle. That is a halo around a neck.
The distance between this house and that house:
where I find an ambulance parked on my street.

This is the victory over the radio, the cheers
along the balcony. This is the small window
in which I mattered and this is the streamer.

UNIVERSITY OF AIR

I took a train and when the doors slid open
I felt the wind. Would I have to live again tomorrow?

I spent the night practicing for the long nap.
I saw a statue of myself: arms straight, head

tilted, lips pursed. I was a splendid person.
I pinched a butterfly on a branch and ate it.

Duck River started spilling over into Pillow Park.
I woke up the way I interrupt a mirror.

I walked outside and drew a tree upon a tree.
I lost my faith in my common sense.

I drove an ice cream truck into the guardrail.
Whoa, I said, you hear everything you say.

REPLICAS OF GRACE

A child apes adults.

An adult wishes
he were more childlike.
Where a kingdom?

Secretly I've come this far.
Out of the forests
of saying "good morning."

A newborn orange
wafts in the terminal air.
One idea: I make
the fruit tree more rare.

The more hosts,
the more pressure on the guest.

THE INTERROGATION

Island, why did you come?
You could have left for good.
But I'm traceable to you.
(I said nothing about you.)

Island, where did you go?
I was told you were here.
I have lived here for years.
But you were not there.

Island, what did you do?
I want to shut you down.
But I know I cannot.
I said nothing about you.

A MEMOIR

He found a single-way of being:

the moon on earth.

No one can verify me.

Look, I have a special disease.

Everyone was always wrong.

That's how he calibrated his answers.

It's been a year or seven.

The days are done moving through him.

Even sleeping, he looks alive.

DEATH POEMS

1

Star chant   star chant
As evening   lightened
Star chant   star chant
The sky unhooked   star chant
Star chant   a single star
Star chant   star chant

2

The suited man from the high-rise
falls, turning over in the air.
His back, then his side, back,
the front of the man as he falls.

3

Speeding on the skyway
my body in the side-seat
I imagine a view from
the curb: my naked self
upright, folded at the lap,
zipping over pavement
dreaming such a person
could do this: inches
from the wall, waking.

4

I've been like a word
cut from a haiku. Now death
brings back my rigor.

5

The rain came down like so many depth charges.
The rain came down like a depth charge.
Each drop came down like a depth charge.
Each drop a depth charge.

6

I went to my
teacher and said,
Master, how do I
write a poem?
He said, Inside one poem
there may be
a great poem.
Inside a great poem,
there may be
many shitty poems.
Then he said, Go,
sit outside
until you see the trees
have throats.
Then he said, Go,
do not ask
for my death poem.

7

Maybe the prayer comes
in the form of an order.
And indeed, he leaped
hoping to die on impact—
not for the ground to recede
before him forever.

8

So many feelings toward Death!

9

Moon's been making
some bold claims tonight.
Car filling up with our bodies.
Kim keeps driving faster,
as if to slow down
might make us disappear.

10

As for death,
stone exists.

11

Should the mongoose burn
like a fire and live
thereafter, he should
burn out like a fire
and thereby leave no trace.

12

You are dead. The Void
welcomes you. You have been here
all along anyway. Your corpse
will get a haircut. The wind
makes a mold of your body.
Doctors gesture around your body.
Your pulse begins again.
You must return. (Are you terrified?)
The world welcomes you anyway.

THE SAD WHOLE

He is composed of infinite acts.
Examine him from the outside
and you'll see he doesn't think.

He was a wild boar and inside
that boar he was a lilac bush.
These things alive within him.

He always moves and through
that moving he is always still.
And he contains and is composed

of the figure of a man himself.
You may feel at home with him
and breathe more fully now.

If we are of his gestures,
there is no one to forgive.

HWAN'S CONDITION

He wants to sleep
but he has to do
all this work, but
he wants to do
all this work, but
he has to sleep.

DREAM TRIAL

1

While thinking of a summer job
I saw a bright flyer on a bulletin board.
Next thing I knew I was on a cruise.
Two minutes before my break,
I saw a bit of commotion
down at the other end of the pool.
She lives across the road from me,
where her family raises llamas.
I knew I was in for a real thrill.
Then my whole vacation got ruined
when I was held for ransom.
Suddenly a big thud happened in the rear.
Can you say heaven on earth?
You have an idea what it was like.
Let's see, I could be a factory worker
at my father's blue-cheese company
or live at the youth hostel in the Twin Cities.
I woke up to a strange surprise.
I emerged from my cannonball
only to find someone had thrown
my clothes on the roof.

2

Some animals live so briefly
they never need to eat. Nothing

indifferent inside your dream.
You want to touch death

without death touching you.
Waking is an emergency.

3

No, no, it's alright.

Hey, no—it's alright.

4

The rain strikes me continuously
until I forget about it. My host mom
wants to sleep with me. Teachers still awake,
patrolling. The train arrives at 7:30—
but on which night? The passenger eager
to arrive or to go through me? I won't be sure
until I meet him, stop him in his tracks.

5

Dusk and snow come at me simultaneously.
She puts down her book bag to hold me.

I convince her I don't love her just by looking.
This part of the dream exhibition.

6

There is a tension between us
like two halves of a metaphor:

similar enough to notice,
different enough to care.

7

A dying girl is not a waterfall.

But if I could show you . . .

Where do I put this?

To not set it down?

8

A bridge where a girl revives her driver.
The driver not wanting to be revived.
The bridge named in this way.

9

Have a drink in the Central City.
The best solution is three solutions!

10

Clouds pass over, watching us,
what shapes we take. The windows

were so articulate today—
and then someone left them open.

Where do I defend my dreams?
Point at my nights.

11

The stagecoach resembles a teahouse
in which I've fallen asleep. The stagecoach
overturned in the canyon. Horses on their sides
crying out. Echoing back and forth inside the ravine.
Morning but the sun is not out.
The driver dead. A little girl survives.
She's not sure where to go. She doesn't know the canyon.
She stays near the body. Charged with questions.

12

What if only my anxieties keep me alive?

What if only my anxieties transmigrate?

13

With the speed of a box
she takes me into a white field.

We touch each other's eyelids.
Telephone poles are all around.

Some people on a fishing boat
can probably see us. Stars

start arriving and at first
we are frightened by the light.

14

Rithy returns to the Hotel Kartika Plaza
located behind the police station
in central Jakarta. She undresses and washes
only one breast. The evening rioters are just waking.
She orders ice and they come to her
with two cubes on a tray. She walks to the window.
She walks to the wall, pressing her ear to the paint.

15

A rioter throws me a stone—
it is smooth in some places, puffed out in others.

16

A dog swims into a field.
I shoot him. I shoot him again.

My uncle puts his barrel
into the wound and fires.

Dog's head halves open
bleeding—his snout up at me

asking me what to do.

17

Let's all start with the same sin
and see what happens! Hey,
what's up? Where are the cups?

18

Easy to cross the river if you are part river.

19

She stays near the body.
Her whole life twisted into a clearing:
serious boys playing baseball,
running sideways in uniforms.
They train themselves at every moment.

20

Rithy's body: an authentic replica
windblown and tattery—unrolls

as a sleeping bag—old trope of death.
The sun will set several times today.

A ham radio buzzes faintly, but
still audibly in the fog—these whispered images,

to burn them all by waking.

21

One can forget about sex
if one imagines the liver,
lungs, spleen and blood.

I can't imagine anything anymore.
I feel like there are cameras on me,
clicking while I eat and sleep.

22

I burn my house and mostly
the people in it. Others watch
so I pass the matches around.

23

I beat a man with the butt of my gun.
I aim for the cul-de-sac.

24

I am the opposite of a solipsist.

25

Six men in wool suits
step neatly into my brownstone.

One says, I'm the co-captain.
You have to see the Coach.

I walk to the sports trailer
they have waiting. Coach says

I'm on trial for my dreams.
I keep trying to wake up.

This all part of the evidence.
Coach says he's dying.

No one talks to him anymore.
As if to talk to a dying man

about his illness you speed up
his dying. Coach takes out the form

for punishment. Says sign it.
Here, he says, here is a sport coat

made of thorns. I sign my name
but secretly mean something else.

26

Each idea we are
pulled off the world
attached now
to a new terrain
where you walk
toward the sun
haunted by the ground,
and I dig into it,
cursing aloud
heaving dirt
into the air, trying
to dig away
what we walk on
and the ground
falls back to itself
and we stand together
pouting at the earth.

27

It may be okay if I love you
as I love the name of a former student.

28

A watermelon grows up in our minds.
We reach in for its sugary flesh.
Marsupials slicing paths in the snow-lot.

Don't leave, I'm taking off my shirt.
When you spin, as in a kitchen,
always focus on some point

far away, and return your gaze to it
after each spin to keep your balance.

29

I lie down on the splintery lawn.
Sparrows 'round me like corners.
Above: a small re-release of rain.
No one can stop the Spring from coming.

Fence Books

THE MOTHERWELL PRIZE

Aim Straight at the Fountain and Press Vaporize	Elizabeth Marie Young
Unspoiled Air	Kaisa Ullsvik Miller

THE ALBERTA PRIZE

The Cow	Ariana Reines
Practice, Restraint	Laura Sims
A Magic Book	Sasha Steensen
Sky Girl	Rosemary Griggs
The Real Moon of Poetry and Other Poems	Tina Brown Celona
Zirconia	Chelsey Minnis

FENCE MODERN POETS SERIES

Star in the Eye	James Shea
Structure of the Embryonic Rat Brain	Christopher Janke
The Stupefying Flashbulbs	Daniel Brenner
Povel	Geraldine Kim
The Opening Question	Prageeta Sharma
Apprehend	Elizabeth Robinson
The Red Bird	Joyelle McSweeney

NATIONAL POETRY SERIES

Collapsible Poetics Theater	Rodrigo Toscano

ANTHOLOGIES & CRITICAL WORKS

*Not for Mothers Only: Contemporary Poets on Child-Getting &
Child-Rearing*   Catherine Wagner & Rebecca Wolff, editors

POETRY

The Method	Sasha Steensen
The Orphan & Its Relations	Elizabeth Robinson
Site Acquisition	Brian Young
Rogue Hemlocks	Carl Martin
19 Names for Our Band	Jibade Khalil Huffman
Infamous Landscapes	Prageeta Sharma
Bad Bad	Chelsey Minnis
Snip Snip!	Tina Brown Celona
Yes, Master	Michael Earl Craig
Swallows	Martin Corless-Smith
Folding Ruler Star	Aaron Kunin
The Commandrine & Other Poems	Joyelle McSweeney
Macular Hole	Catherine Wagner
Nota	Martin Corless-Smith
Father of Noise	Anthony McCann
Can You Relax in My House	Michael Earl Craig
Miss America	Catherine Wagner

FICTION

Flet: A Novel	Joyelle McSweeney
The Mandarin	Aaron Kunin